Nicolas POUSSIN
Masterpieces 1594-1665

'I AM UNABLE TO RID MY MIND OF THOSE PAINTINGS' BERNINI

Nicolas POUSSIN
Masterpieces 1594-1665

Pierre Rosenberg
Président Directeur, the Louvre, Paris

and

Véronique Damian

translated by
Sophie Henley-Price with Michael Worton

CASSELL

DESIGNED BY
Ariane Aubert

TRANSLATED FROM THE FRENCH BY
Sophie Henley-Price with Michael Worton

Front cover
The Triumph of Venus, 1634 (detail),
Philadelphia, Philadelphia Museum of Art.

First published in the UK 1995 by Cassell
Villiers House, 41/47 Strand, London WC2N 5JE

French original published as *Nicolas Poussin*
Copyright © Somogy Editions D'Art 1994
English translation © Somogy Editions D'Art 1995

Distributed in Australia
by Capricorn Link (Australia) Pty Ltd
2/13 Carrington Road, Castle Hill NSW 2154

British Library Cataloguing-in-Publication Data
A catalogue record for this book is available from the British Library

ISBN 0-304-34537-7

'I have neglected nothing'

'For goodness sake, you cannot in the same breath talk about a painter like Monet, who is quite simply a genius, and an old, untalented, cliché-ridden artist like Poussin. I will be totally frank in saying that I find him the most tedious of all bores. What else can I say, I really cannot call that painting. Monet, Degas, Manet, yes, there you have real painters.' (Proust, *À la recherche du temps perdu*). This judgment, uttered by Madame de Cambremer, will find few supporters today! For Poussin is unquestionably one of the most important seventeenth-century painters. He did not have the dazzling career of a Rubens or a Velazquez, both of whom had the gift of profitably allying their prolific output with their social standing. His artistic aim was very different: painting whose 'aim is delectation.' Poussin believed that 'verisimilitude and judgment' were essential to a painter and he wrote on the eve of his death: 'They are like Virgil's Golden Bough which none can find or pick, unless driven by Destiny.' Was it destiny which first drove Poussin from his native Normandy to Paris, and then on to Rome in 1624? Here, at all events, he settled and remained until his death in 1665, with the exception of an unfortunate two-year return in Paris.

The early years

Little is known of Poussin's early life, from his birth at Les Andelys in June 1594 until his arrival in Rome in 1624. The artist himself kept a veil of secrecy over his early years. His biographers have left us with indications of an early vocational calling which appeared to have been encouraged by the painter Quentin Varin (1570-1634) during his short stay in Les Andelys in 1612. Indeed, that very year Poussin quietly left the family home and made his way to Paris. His artistic training came in two stages: for a month he worked under Georges Lallemant (*c.*1575-1636), and he then studied for three months under Ferdinand Elle (*c.*1580-1649), although he also appears to have acquired a solid classical training along the way. Light has been thrown on the period between the ages of twenty and twenty-eight, frequently called 'the unknown years', by the recent discovery in the *Archives Nationales* of two deeds which offer new facts and useful clarification. The first is a covenant of debt for the sum of 120 livres (the equivalent of nine months' living costs) dated 10 June 1619 and owed to Jean Guillemin, a merchant goldsmith established in the rue St-Germain-l'Auxerrois. By then, Poussin was already referred to as a painter living close to the Louvre and having a comfortable standard of living. The second deed, dated 23 August 1622, states that Poussin had still not reimbursed the debt. We know that prior to his departure from Paris at the end of 1623 Poussin had already made two unsuccessful attempts to reach Rome, once getting as far as Florence and the other ending at Lyon. It may be that Poussin had to pay back Jean Guillemin all the money he had set aside for his second trip to Italy. According to his biographers, the journey ended in Lyon for that very reason. This theory was put forward by Jacques Thuillier and is indeed a very attractive one. In 1622, Poussin's return to Paris coincided with the canonization of Ignatius Loyola and Francis Xavier, as a result of which the Jesuit College, in order to mark the celebrations, commissioned from him six paintings, now lost.

Rome, artistic capital of Europe

In the spring of 1624, after breaking his journey in Venice, Poussin arrived in the Eternal City, where the Rome of classical antiquity and contemporary Rome stood juxtaposed: the dome of St Peter's, the Capitol, and other works of Michelangelo were considered to be fully equal to the monuments of the past. The new Baroque era was in full flower during the pontificate of Urban VIII (1623-1644), a Barberini, and under him Rome was transformed into a vast building site. As early as 1623, Bernini was made responsible for the redecoration of St Peter's, to which Poussin was able to make a contribution, receiving a commission for one of the altars: *The Martyrdom of St Erasmus* (1628; Vatican, Vatican Museums). It was the period when large-scale figures dominated and occupied all the space in his paintings, for example in *The Inspiration of the*

The Virgin appearing to St James, 1629-1630.
Oil on canvas, 301 x 242 cm. Paris, Louvre.

Poet (Paris, Louvre), or *The Virgin appearing to St James* (Paris, Louvre), a painting which later artists such as David were to recall in their work. Urban VIII was a francophile and numerous French artists took up residence in Rome as a result, notably Simon Vouet who arrived in 1613 and stayed until 1627. It is equally important to note that Poussin's first major work executed in Rome, *The Death of Germanicus* (1627), was carried out for one of the Pope's nephews, Cardinal Francesco Barberini. However, the prestige of these two commissions should not detract from the hardships and privations encountered during these early Roman years; his serious illness (probably syphilis) from which he recovered through the good care of a French cook, Jacques Dughet, one of whose daughters, Anne-Marie, married Poussin in 1630. By then he was thirty-six years old and his life was changing and beginning to have some real structure to it. From 1631 to

The Nurture of Jupiter, 1638-1640.
Oil on canvas, 97 x 133 cm.
Berlin, Staatliche Museen zu Berlin, Gemäldegalerie.

1635, his brother-in-law, Gaspard Dughet, trained with him and shared the couple's home. Poussin had no studio despite the rapidly increasing number of commissions resulting from the patronage of the Barberini family and Cassiano dal Pozzo. His modest home was in the Via Paolina, in a district which stretched from the Piazza del Popolo to the Piazza di Spagna, an area popular with foreign artists living in Rome. There he led a peaceful life, favourable to the study of classical antiquity and to the study of the nude, first at the Academy of Domenichino and then in the studio of Andrea Sacchi, but he also discovered the joy of painting the Roman Campagna in the company of Claude Gellée and Sandrart. In addition to his Roman patrons, commissions also arrived from France where his friend, the painter Jacques Stella, who had returned to Paris in 1634, would order paintings from him and then set about making them known. *The Nurture of Jupiter* (1638) was the first painting carried out for Paul Fréart de Chantelou, his main French patron and friend. Indeed by 1638, his reputation in Paris was so well established that the King of France himself set about tempting the artist back. On 17 December 1640, after protracted negotiations, Poussin reluctantly arrived in Paris.

*Poussin: 'Premier peintre ordinaire du roi' ***

The artist was afforded a welcome which matched all promises and all expectations. Louis XIII allocated him an income of 3,000 livres a year and a house in the Tuileries. In exchange, Poussin accepted responsibility for the preparation of the designs for the redecoration of the Grande Galerie at the Louvre; Sublet de Noyers, Richelieu's principal artistic adviser, had previously assured him that he would paint neither 'ceilings nor vaults.' Indeed, Poussin had no experience of frescoes and very little of working on a large scale, preferring to paint at the easel. Nevertheless, for the royal chapel of St-Germain-en-Laye, he executed *The Institution of the Eucharist* (Paris, Louvre), which was said to have given the king and queen 'as much pleasure as did the sight of their children.' Other commissions for Cardinal Richelieu and for Sublet de Noyers followed. For Richelieu he executed *Moses and the Burning Bush* (Copenhagen, Statens Museum for Kunst) and a ceiling painting on canvas, *Time Saving Truth from Envy and Discord* (Paris, Louvre); for Sublet de Noyers, who was the founding patron of the church of the Jesuit novitiate in Paris, another large altarpiece depicting *The*

* *'First painter to the king'*

Time saving Truth from Envy and Discord, 1641.
Oil on canvas, diameter 297 cm.
Paris, Louvre.

Miracle of St Francis Xavier (Paris, Louvre). Poussin worked hastily and reluctantly. He was uncomfortable executing works on such a huge scale and the project of the Grande Galerie brought him very little satisfaction. However, the death of the exiled Marie de Médicis on 3 July 1642 and the war against the Protestants were precursors of major political upheavals in France. Art became secondary to intrigue and war, and Poussin was determined to return to Rome, where he arrived on 5 November 1642. The death of Richelieu in 1642 and that shortly afterwards of Louis XIII in 1643 were pretexts enough for him never to return to France.

The Miracle of St Francis Xavier, 1641.
Oil on canvas, 444 x 234 cm. Paris, Louvre.

A lonely furrow

For Poussin, the transition from Rome to Paris was comparable to having gone 'from heaven to hell'. He loved to create in peace and solitude with all the time and reflection artistic creation required, hence his reputation as a painter-philosopher. He took pleasure in reminding Chantelou that he was not 'like your painters in Paris who will make you a painting in the space of twenty-four hours.' Nor was he interested in adopting the baroque style of a Pietro da Cortona who specialized in executing huge ceiling paintings. Poussin had no studio, hence he had no apprentices (other than his brother-in-law Gaspard Dughet) nor any direct followers. At the very most, he had some imitators. After his unsatisfactory Parisian interlude, he then had twenty-three prolific years, withdrawn from the public domain, indifferent alike to honours and envious ill-wishers. His art, imbued with philosophical meditation, was marked by a stoicism which is reflected in the second series of *Sacraments* which he painted for Chantelou. He created powerful, perfectly balanced compositions which expressed human tragedies, such as *The Judgment of Solomon* (1649), but also resulted in some of the finest seventeenth-century landscapes: *The Funeral* and *The Ashes of Phocion* or, equally, *Pyramus and Thisbe,*

The Storm and *Orion*. Furthermore, for the duc de Richelieu, great-nephew of the cardinal, he undertook the *Four Seasons* (1660-1664), his 'artistic and spiritual testament.' With old age approaching, Poussin's interest progressively turned towards the grandeur of nature which he endeavoured to reproduce with the greatest possible accuracy. He continued to turn down offers of public honours, refusing the title of 'Prince' of the Academy of St Luke in November 1657. Determined to paint right up to his last moments, he fought against his trembling hands and his illness, about which he had already begun to complain as early as 1642. The moving passage in his famous letter dated July 1663 bears witness to this personal struggle: 'It is with great difficulty that I reply to you, due to the weakness of my shaking hand which no longer obeys my will, as you can see [...] I have laid aside my brushes forever, and my only thoughts are of dying, death being the sole cure for the ills which afflict me. May God let it be soon, as life weighs too heavily upon me...'

Anne-Marie was the first to die, towards the end of 1664, after nine months of illness. Poussin outlived her by a year and did 'little else other than drink, for the sheer pleasure, an occasional small glass of fine wine with his neighbour Claude Lorrain,' as Abraham Bruegel wrote in a letter dated 22 April 1665. Poussin

Poussin's tomb in Rome.

died on 19 November 1665, having settled his inheritance, albeit with some difficulty. In accordance with the wishes of the artist, his body was transported 'in all simplicity' to the parish church of San Lorenzo in Lucina and buried after a sung High Mass.

The painter left behind him an inheritance of 15,000 crowns which may indeed seem little in comparison to the 40,000 crowns left by his contemporary, Pietro da Cortona. In reality, however, it represented a sum which would have allowed the artist to live more comfortably than he chose to do. Hence the insistent reminders on the part pf his biographers that Poussin had no servants and preferred 'the tranquility and comfort of his small home,' and the discretion of an ordered life, to all the honours of the world.

'One day I asked him how he had attained the mastery that had granted him such an exalted place among the great painters of Italy. To this he modestly answered: "I neglected nothing".' This moving testimony recorded by the painter Abraham Bruegel fittingly emphasises the great discipline with which Poussin approached all aspects of his art.

Landscape with Three Men, 1650-1651.
Oil on canvas, 120 x 187 cm. Madrid, Museo del Prado.

The Death of Germanicus

Two years after arriving in Rome in 1624, Poussin was awarded a commission by Cardinal Francesco Barberini, nephew of Pope Urban VIII. He tackled a subject from ancient Roman history, drawn from the *Annals* of Tacitus (II, *LXXI* and *LXXII*). Germanicus, a noble general who took his name from his numerous victories in the German campaigns, fell ill at Antioch, probably poisoned on the orders of his adoptive father, the Emperor Tiberius. On his deathbed, he called together his family, friends and generals; some swore to avenge him but he asked his wife that she '...lay aside her pride and bend her soul to the vagaries of Fate.' In the painting the two groups stand opposed to each other: one soldier swears revenge with a declamatory gesture of his right hand while in contrast Germanicus' wife and children are sunk in attitudes of despair. Pointing to his family, Germanicus appears to be addressing his generals. The frieze-like composition is inspired by ancient

Oil on canvas, 148 x 198 cm, 1627.
Minneapolis, The Minneapolis Institute of Arts.

sculpture (notably the sarcophagus in *The Death of Meleager*, now at Wilton House, near Salisbury) but, most importantly, the arrangement allows the artist to portray a large number of figures without any impression of disorder. A preliminary sketch and the evidence of an X-ray of the painting indicate that the composition was carefully planned. Initially, the artist painted neither the soldier raising his right arm in the foreground nor the enclosed architecture of the background, but instead a stairway open to the sky. No doubt Poussin was well aware of the importance of this commission at a difficult moment in his career, shortly after his arrival in Rome. He could never have suspected the immense influence the painting would have, culminating in *The Oath of the Horatii* (1785) by David (Paris, Louvre) and the history painting of neo-classical artists in general.

The Massacre of the Innocents

The Massacre of the Innocents has no equivalent elsewhere in Poussin's work. It is unique for several reasons: the ambition of the composition, the novelty of approach to the subject and the concentration of narrative. This episode from the New Testament, at the time of the Flight into Egypt, is the consequence of the wrath of Herod, who in his attempt to find and kill the baby Jesus, '...sent forth, and slew all the children that were in Bethlehem, and in all the coasts thereof, from two years old and under.' Normally, for example in the composition by Raphael, this particularly cruel massacre is portrayed by a confusion of soldiers, mothers and dead children strewn on the ground. Poussin's characterization is quite the reverse : stark clarity and simplicity dominate, further accentuating the horror of the deed. Arranged theatrically, the triangular group in the foreground of soldier, mother and child is in itself sufficient to explain the action; although a few weeping women cradle their dead children in the background, they would not in themselves explain the scene, as there are no soldiers present. Poussin has framed these unusually large-scale figures against an austere architectural background. No compromise is made: the young mother, deathly pale, her features frozen like an ancient tragic mask, the distraught young woman in the immediate background, howling her grief as she rushes away from the scene, face lifted towards heaven as the body of the little child, pinned under a soldier's foot, already spurts blood; all this serves to increase the spectator's sense of horror at the massacre. Who could have commissioned from Poussin this painting which, whilst drawing inspiration from its precursors (Marcantonio's engraving after Raphael, or the painting by Poussin's Bolognese contemporary, Guido Reni, in the Pinacoteca Nazionale in Bologna), differs so radically from them? The work is first mentioned in 1638 in the inventory drawn up after the death of Marquese Vincenzo Giustiniani (1564-1637) as part of a series above doors, including three other paintings depicting subjects associated with morality and death: the *Death of Seneca* by Joachim von Sandrart, the *Death of Cicero* by François Perrier and, finally, the *Death of Socrates* by a certain 'Giusto fiammengo.' Although it is an early work (*c.*1627-1628), when it is seen in its true historical and artistic context *The Massacre of the Innocents* can be recognised as a work of great moral weight and authority. Three centuries later it was to function as one of the main visual sources for Picasso's *Guernica*.

Oil on canvas, 147 x 171 cm, *c.*1627-1628.
Chantilly, Musée Condé.

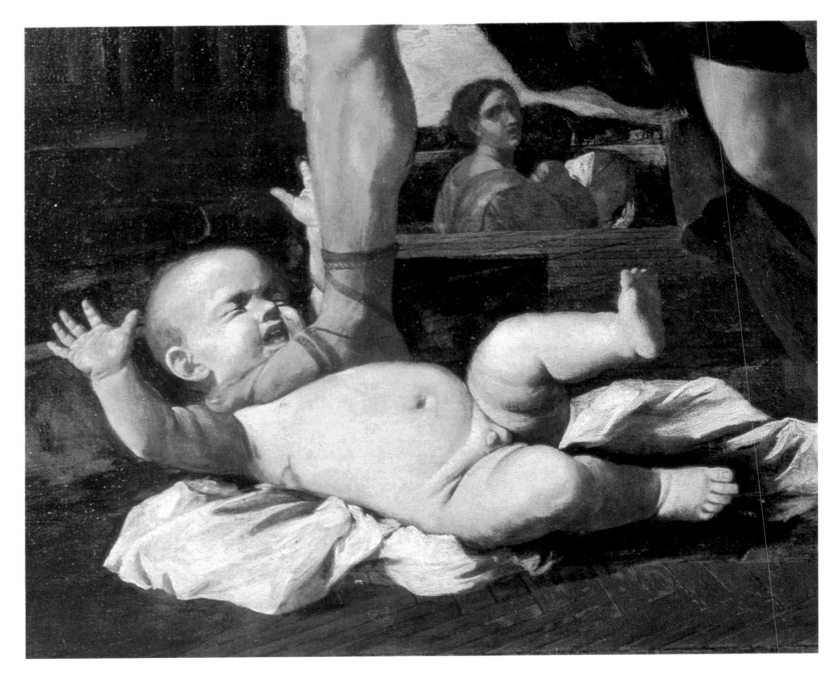

'Throughout French painting and until
Guernica, *no woman had ever screamed*
as loudly as that mother had.'
(*Jacques Thuillier, 1961*).

The Triumph of David

For this well-worked theme, Poussin chose to depict not the story of the fight itself, when the young shepherd David, in the name of the God of Israel, kills the giant Goliath by striking him on the forehead with a stone from his sling, but rather the episode that follows, the celebration of victory. Having beheaded the Philistine Goliath with the giant's own sword, the young David, portrayed as a hero rather than as a shepherd, sits pensively beside the corpse and is crowned by a semi-naked Victory, a figure more pagan than biblical. She removes his wreath of oak leaves, and replaces it with a royal crown, alluding to the destiny awaiting him as the son of Jesse. Leaning on Goliath's sword, dressed in a toga, David is turned, somewhat abstractedly, towards the severed head of the defeated Philistine. The right hand side of the composition, evoking

war, stands in contrast to the left hand side where a small infant is playing with an aeolian harp. Tradition has it that David owned such an instrument, whose distinctive particularity was that a night breeze set it humming by itself. This skilful and scholarly allusion confirms Poussin's learned knowledge of Roman archeology, as testified by many of his paintings. The shafts of the fluted columns define an architectural space which once again refers back to Antiquity – in the same manner as the winged Victory draws its inspiration from a sculpted figure on the base of an antique relief in the Doria-Pamphili collection in Rome. The subtle silvery grey tones of the painting contribute to the intro-spective nature of the work which seems to have been executed shortly after the completion of *The Death of Germanicus* in 1628.

Oil on canvas, 100 x 130 cm, 1628.
Madrid, Museo del Prado.

Through the act of replacing the wreath of oak leaves with a royal crown, Victory clearly anticipates the future which awaits David, as the son of Jesse.

Tancred and Erminia

'(*Erminia and Vafrin) had reached the outskirts of the town/at the time when the East darkens with the setting sun/when they came upon ground soaked in blood:/ then they perceived a dead warrior amidst the blood/ lying across the width of the road, his face/turned towards the sky, menacing even in death.*' So the scene is set for this subject taken from Tasso's *Gerusalemme Liberata* (XIX, 101-113). In this first version of the painting, now in the Hermitage, Poussin is absolutely faithful to the time of day described by Tasso, rendering exquisitely the warm twilight which envelops the dramatic moment. Erminia recognizes the wounded Tancred, who has just fought in single combat against Argant whose body lies behind to the right, noticeable only because of the reflections on his armour, but she does not know how to dress his wounds in this desert: '*She dries his wounds with her*

hair which she has chosen to cut.' This she does with Tancred's sword, the gesture being Poussin's idea, as is Erminia's mysterious horse which gazes on the melancholy scene. In this masterpiece of visual poetry, lightly painted with the tip of the brush, there is a masterly interplay of shade and reflection.

'The painter has created a story more beautiful than the poet,' asserted Jonathan Richardson Jr who knew the Birmingham version, brought back to England in 1717 by the painter-decorator James Thornhill. This second version was painted four or five years after the one in the Hermitage, in around 1634. The atmosphere here is completely different. The elegiac and romantic spirit has given way to a more clearly set out narrative and a more solid and disciplined structure. The scene is more compact, the essence

Oil on canvas, 98 x 147 cm, *c.*1630.
St Petersburg, Hermitage Museum.

of the story being conveyed rather than any anecdotal detail, the characters being given greater importance and occupying the foreground. Argant has taken the place of the beautiful white horse of the first version, and the two small cupids carrying torches remind us that love is an integral part of the story. Poussin has again included Erminia's act of devotion, as she cuts off her hair to dress the wounds of the man she loves. Closer to Tancred, she has removed his upper clothing to examine his injuries; more intent on her task, she is now kneeling, whilst Vafrin gently lifts the wounded body. Poussin adopts a binary rhythm: the confrontation of the two protagonists echoed by the two warriors stretched out on the ground, the two horses and, in the background, the two tree trunks. The colours, now lighter, are more clearly contrasted.

Oil on canvas, 75 x 100 cm, *c.*1634.
Birmingham, Barber Institute of Fine Arts.

'Vafrin said to her: "He is not dead: / so let us heal him before mourning him." / He rids him of his armour [...] / She dries his wounds with her hair and dresses them / with that same hair which she has chosen to cut.'
(Tasso, Gerusalemme Liberata)

The Martyrdom of St Erasmus

The Martyrdom of St Erasmus was commissioned in February 1628 for an altar in the transept of St Peter's in Rome. It was the only major ecclesiastical commission which Poussin managed to secure before his work on the huge altarpieces in Paris in the early 1640s, and was destined to replace another painting on the subject of the martyrdom of St Erasmus, Bishop of Gaeta, burned and doused in boiling oil. Poussin decided to use the fourteenth-century version of the legend which speaks of the saint's intestines being drawn out on a windlass (one of the earliest representations of this version is in Gaeta Cathedral). St Erasmus, whose torture is already well advanced, has still the option of renouncing his faith and offering sacrifice to the pagan idols. The high priest, dressed in white, is pointing to the statue of Hercules whilst his assistants wait for an answer, and the executioner impassively turns the crank. The vertical format determines the structure of a restricted space in which the figures are moving one in front of the other. The overlapping group of the two assistants and an onlooker shows striking contrasts of red and blue.

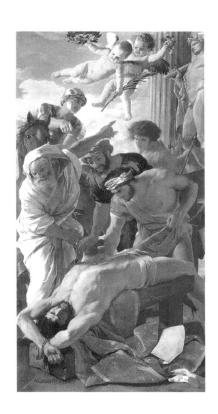

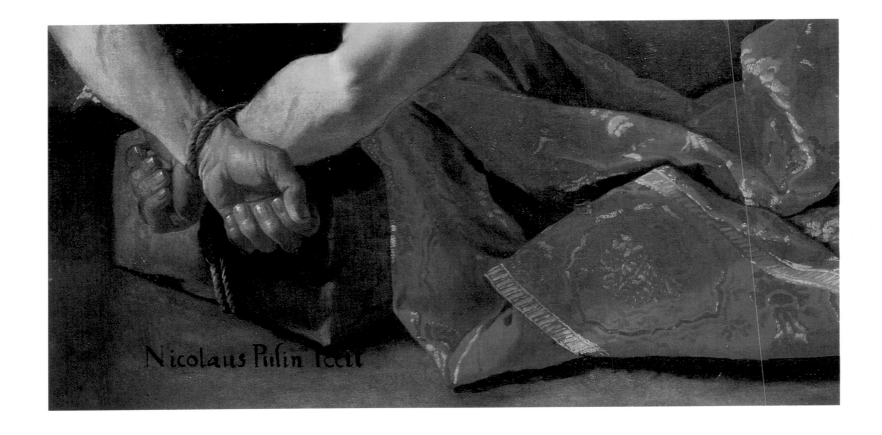

Poussin only very rarely signed his works. The Martyrdom of St Erasmus *is the first of his paintings in which he departed from this tradition, incorporating his signature in Latin.*

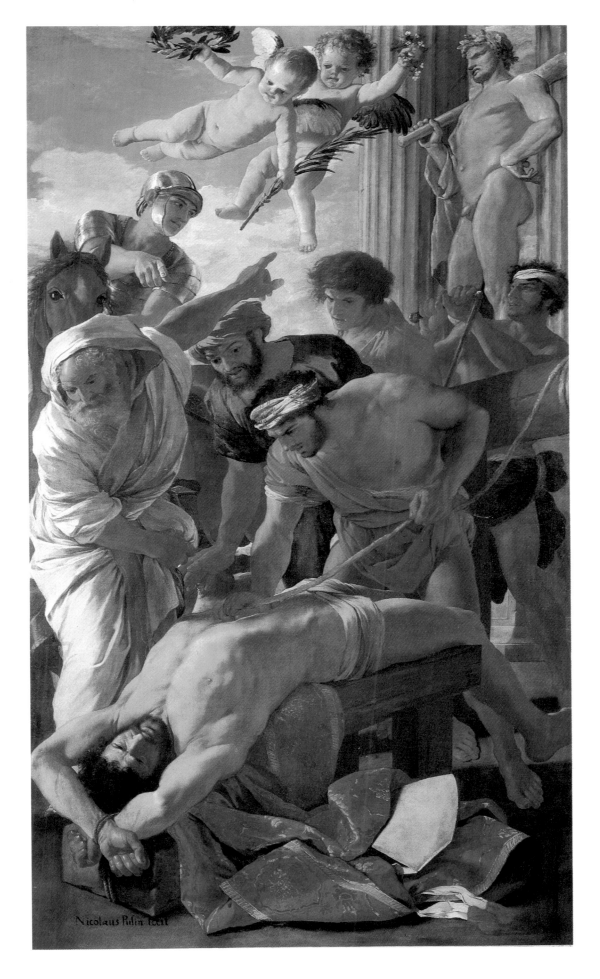

Oil on canvas, 320 x 186 cm,
1628-1629.
Vatican, Vatican Museums.

Echo and Narcissus

The nymph Echo, painted with a light hand by the artist, seems to have merged with the rock on which she sadly reclines, all hope gone.

The prophet Tiresias had predicted to Liriope, the mother of Narcissus, that her son would live for 'many years, to a great old age' on the rather mysterious condition that 'he know not himself.' Narcissus remains indifferent to all the passionate love aroused by his beauty. The resentment felt by the nymph Echo, one of the 'victims of his disdain,' leads her to wish 'that he in turn should love in the same way but never possess the object of his love.' One day, tired by a day's hunting, the young man lies down beside a spring and falls in love with his own reflection in the water. This impossible and barren love leads him to waste away and finally to die, the victim of the inexorable destiny foreseen by Tiresias.

This painting is totally faithful to the episode recounted in Ovid's *Metamorphoses* (III, 339-510), on which Poussin drew for a great number of his subjects. The artist brings together several episodes from the narrative: the death of Narcissus, the moment when flowers appear in his stead whilst a small cupid (represented here as a funerary spirit) advances with a torch. This passage from the *Metamorphoses* explains how, whilst the pyre was being prepared, the body vanished and a flower, the narcissus, grew in its place. Rather than depicting the well-known moment when the young man first catches sight of his reflection in the water, Poussin has concentrated on conveying Echo's resignation and Narcissus' fated languor which will draw him to his tragic end.

The painting, whose patron remains unknown, was in the collection of Cardinal Angelo Giori in 1669, alongside the *Venus with the dead Adonis* now at the Musée de Caen. The choice of subject and the sensitivity with which it is handled places the painting towards the end of the third decade of the seventeenth century.

Oil on canvas, 74 x 100 cm, *c*.1630.
Paris, Louvre.

Stretched out like 'a statue of Parian marble [...], he drew down his tunic and struck his naked breast with his marble hands' *(Ovid,* Metamorphoses*). Narcissus died whilst still in the full flower of youth, strength and beauty; neither the splendour of nature (represented by the tree in flower) where he loved to hunt nor the love of Echo could prevent him from drifting towards death.*

Phaeton begging the Chariot of Apollo

Of all the subjects taken from Ovid's *Metamorphoses*, this is perhaps the most hermetic. The scene is set in the palace of the Sun, where Apollo sits enthroned in the company of the Days, the Months, the Centuries, the Hours and the Seasons. In this painting, only the latter are represented by Poussin. Winter, 'all of ice with a head of tangled white hair,' is most faithful to Ovid's description. Summer holds a glowing mirror, and sheaves of wheat lie at her feet; Spring has 'her head wreathed with flowers' and Autumn lies somnolent under the influence of wine. Time is represented by Saturn who presents Apollo with the Mirror of Truth. Surrounded by the circle of the zodiac, the Sun God welcomes his mortal son, Phaeton, who has come to demand that Apollo prove his paternal love by allowing him to drive the sun chariot for a day. Apollo tries to dissuade him, but in vain. The nymphs are already harnessing the horses, their solemn expression suggesting the tragic outcome. The artist has tempered this piece of visual scholarship with light, almost translucent, shades. The painting is contemporaneous with *Echo and Narcissus*, around 1630.

The skilful arrangement of the Seasons, who are grouped in a semi-circle around Apollo, evokes the path of the sun, here represented by the Sun God himself.

NICOLAS POUSSIN

*Phaeton begging the Chariot of Apollo, c.*1630.
Oil on canvas, 122 x 153 cm.
Berlin, Staatliche Museen, Gemäldegalerie.

The Plague at Ashdod

We are able to date this painting from the evidence Poussin gave on 27 July 1631 at the trial of Fabrizio Valguarnera, a Neapolitan diamond dealer who had bought the painting from him. Started towards the end of 1630, it was delivered to Valguarnera in March 1631. In January 1632, Valguarnera died in prison in mysterious circumstances, the painting having already been sold on for the enormous sum of 1,000 crowns. The scandal had undoubtedly added to its value, and it continued to be greatly admired, being purchased around 1660 by the duc de Richelieu. The painting found its way into the collection of Louis XIV five years later.

The episode depicted is referred to in the first book of Samuel (V, 1-6). The Israelites had been defeated by the Philistines who took the Ark of the God of Israel to Ashdod and placed it in their temple next to the statue of the god Dagon. Two days later in the morning, the statue (to the left of the painting), had 'fallen upon his face to

the ground before the Ark of the Lord; and the head of Dagon and both the palms of his hands were cut off upon the threshhold. The hand of the Lord was heavy upon them of Ashdod, and he destroyed them, and smote them with tumours,' and the country was devastated by rats. Poussin's ability to interpret a text and transcribe it accurately into a picture is here, as always, astonishing. The spectator is immediately trans-fixed with horror at this town where death spares not a soul and the decaying corpses seem to emit a palpable smell of putrefaction. A pallid light pervades the composition which is filled with references to Raphael and to Sebastiano Serlio's perspective stage designs. In the areas of shadow, the rats, painted very faintly, are barely discernible on the surface of the canvas. In the middle ground, a small group of people shrink away from the temple. Everywhere misery reigns – the con-sequence of so rashly insulting their enemy's God.

'*...having depicted the contagious disease and the distress of the Philistines, he had succeeded in conveying the pervading gloom through the use of a dim light, dark shadows and a languor which could be read in the gestures of every figure present.*'
(Guillet de St Georges, *Compte rendu de la séance de l'Académie de Peinture du 1er mars 1670*).

The Plague at Ashdod, 1631.
Oil on canvas, 148 x 198 cm.
Paris, Louvre.

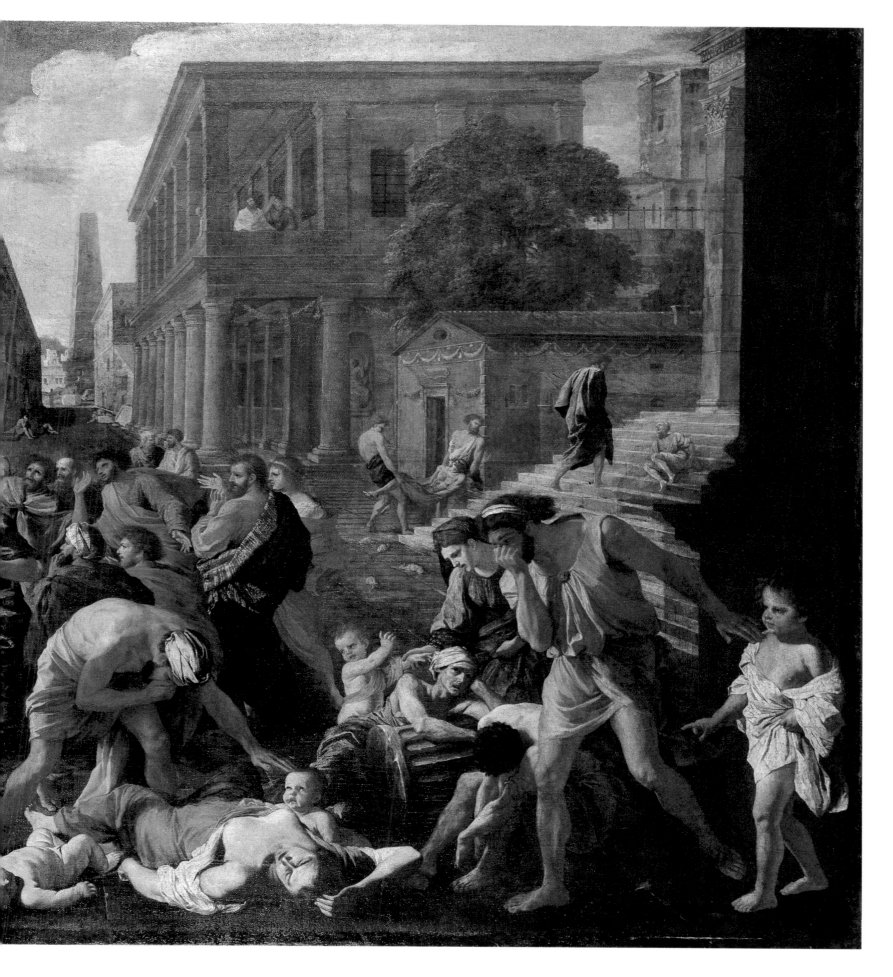

Apollo and the Muses

Whilst turning once again to Ovid's *Metamorphoses* for inspiration, Poussin borrows from and pays tribute to Raphael's fresco *Parnassus* in the Stanza della Segnatura, (Vatican), but draws even greater inspiration from Marcantonio's somewhat different engraving after Raphael. As in the latter's painting, Apollo, seated on Mount Parnassus, is surrounded by nine Muses and nine Poets. From left to right, the muses are divided into two groups. In the first we see Thalia with the mask (Comedy), Urania with the star (Astronomy), Clio with the trumpet (Heroic History and Poetry) and Melpomene who holds a small sword and a mask (Tragedy). In the next group Poussin has painted Terpsichore dancing (Dance), Erato without an instrument but her hand embracing the tree under the cherub carrying his *viola da braccia* (Elegy), Polymnia (Lyrical Poetry), Euterpe carrying flutes (Music) and finally, Calliope (Epic Poetry) crowning the poet. At Apollo's feet, a spring, personified by a nude water nymph, with amphorae, suggests that the location is Mount Helicon, site of the Hippocrene, the spring created by Pegasus, the waters of which engender Inspiration. Apollo holds out a cup to the crowned poet; the two energetic cherubs in the foreground pass round the cups filled directly from the stream.

Who are the Greek poets who here have attained immortality? Barely distinguishable one from the other (although the poetess Sappho's long hair singles her out), they are bringing their work in offering to Apollo. They have come not simply to listen to the enchanting tunes played on the lyre by Apollo, who leans casually on his emblematic instrument, but also to drink at the very source of divine inspiration – which alone can create the 'poetic fury' to which Plato refers. Furthermore, the poets are pointing towards the spring as if to emphasize its creative powers and their dependence upon it.

As an allegory to the glorification of Poetry, the work has been thought to be a hidden reference and tribute paid to Poussin's first great patron, the poet Giambattista Marino, author of

Although there is no documentary proof to support the hypothesis, it is tempting to agree with Panofsky's contention that the poet being crowned with a laurel wreath represents Marino, the great seventeenth-century poet, for whom Poussin illustrated scenes from Ovid's Metamorphoses. *Marino was one of the first in Paris to recognize Poussin's talent and was later of invaluable help when the poor and still unknown artist arrived in Rome in 1624.*

Oil on canvas, 145 x 197 cm, *c.*1631-1632.
Madrid, Museo del Prado.

L'Adone, whom he first met in Paris in 1623 and then in Rome in 1624. But more generally, the painting is a hymn to Inspiration without which no artist can create. Several different interpretations can be advanced for this sophis-ticated and complex painting, which is striking for the brilliance and clarity in its use of colour. It can be dated around 1631-1632, painted at much the same time as the *Empire of Flora*, now in Dresden.

The Triumph of Venus

Despite the assertions of Poussin's early biographers, there is no real indication that this 'sea Bacchanal' was painted for Cardinal Richelieu (who held the office of Navy superintendent) nor that it accompanied three other Bacchanals which the artist executed for him (two in the National Gallery in London, one in the Kansas City Museum). By the same token, there are no surviving documents indicating the circumstances surrounding its commission and even less information on the subject itself, which has given rise to heated debate as to its meaning. Are we faced with a 'Triumph of Galatea,' showing Poussin's debt to Raphael's painting of the same subject (Rome, Villa Farnesina), or rather a 'Birth of Venus,' or perhaps even a 'Triumph of Neptune and Amphitrite.'

Venus occupies the centre of the picture, capturing the attention of the surrounding sea gods and goddesses who are arranged in a semi-circle. The figures, grouped closely together and presented frontally, are approaching the shore with a beautiful, even light bathing their naked bodies and glistening on the dolphins and horses. There is a striking contrast between the astonishing sense of a film-still and the mobility suggested by the wind billowing the drapery into great colourful clouds. Avoiding a frieze-like composition, Poussin here achieves a harmonious rhythm of curves and countercurves, balanced – as with the two giant shells, the chariot of Neptune and the throne of Venus – and occasionally opposed, as with the group of three figures on the right.

In this painting, Poussin, the leading figure of French classicism, applies a very different style, one which is rich in detail and based on a complex network of curves. Whilst recalling Raphael it can also be seen as a timid echo of the baroque compositions of Poussin's contemporary, Pietro da Cortona.

The Triumph of Venus, 1634.
Oil on canvas, 114 x 146 cm.
Philadelphia, Philadelphia Museum of Art.

The Arcadian Shepherds

'Et in Arcadia Ego' or 'Felicity subject to death'

Poussin tackled this subject twice, a gap of about ten years intervening between the two paintings. While the Louvre version is better known, it should not be allowed to overshadow the earlier one at Chatsworth, which was probably painted around 1627.

The identity of the patron of *The Arcadian Shepherds* remains unknown as does that of the proposer of this allegorical subject to Poussin (who may or may not have been the person who commissioned it). The Chatsworth painting is first mentioned in 1677, in the inventory drawn up after the death of Cardinal Camillo Massimi, where it is paired with *Midas washing at the Source of the Pactolus* (New York, The Metropolitan Museum of Art).

The visual source of Poussin's composition is undoubtedly to be found in its famous precedent (*c.*1618, Rome, Galleria Corsini) by the Bolognese painter, Guercino (1591-1666), which, in all likelihood, was painted for the Barberini. Florentine in origin, they were at this time amongst the most important families of patrons in Rome; Cardinal Francesco Barberini, in particular, had commissioned from Poussin *The Death of Germanicus*. One might suggest that it was thanks to the Barberini that the painter became familiar with Guercino's canvas.

The literary sources are numerous: from Virgil's *Eclogues* to Jacopo Sannazaro's *Arcadia* (1502), they conjure an idyllic, imaginary land, 'a kingdom of Utopia.' For his theme Poussin took up the inscription in Guercino's painting *Et in Arcadia Ego*, which Panofsky, in his exemplary study of the two paintings, put forward as meaning 'Even in Arcadia I exist'; 'I' being Death. Two shepherds and their lovely companion, walking in the land of Arcadia, come upon an imposing tomb on which lies a skull. Poussin adds in the river-god of Arcadia, Alpheius. One of the shepherds is deciphering the inscription. The dreamy expression on the young girl's face lends a note of melancholy, which becomes far more grave and solemn in the Louvre version.

Il Guercino, *The Arcadian Shepherds*, *c.*1618. Rome, Galleria Corsini.

The Arcadian Shepherds,
Chatsworth (detail).

The Arcadian Shepherds,
Louvre (detail).

The significance of the skull, the essential element of a memento mori, *discreetly present on the tomb, is reinforced by the Latin inscription* Et in Arcadia Ego, *which projects us into an idyllic world where, nonetheless, death is ever present.*

Oil on canvas, 101 x 82 cm, *c.*1627.
Chatsworth, Devonshire Collection.

Oil on canvas, 85 x 121 cm, *c.*1638.
Paris, Louvre.

As in the first version, the patron of this second 'moral and allegorical contemplation' (Félibien) painted around 1638, remains unknown, but its fate was to be far more prestigious. It entered the collection of Louis XIV in 1685. From the seventeenth to the nineteenth centuries it was immensely popular both with painters, who frequently drew inspiration from this 'eloquent tomb,' and with Romantic poets and writers. In the nine-teenth century, the painting was chosen by Louis Desprez as the model for the bas-relief he created (to a design by Chateaubriand) for the funerary monument to Poussin at San Lorenzo in Lucina.

The Louvre painting, quiet and monumental, reveals a distinct change in style from the works preceding it. Poussin presents us with figures 'who meditate in order to offer us food for thought' and 'one can almost hear these young

people discuss death, which spares neither age nor beauty and from which even the most fortunate of climes furnish no refuge' (Abbé du Bos). Who utters the *Et in Arcadia Ego* here? It is no longer the skull, which some say has been displaced by a scythe created by the shadow of the kneeling shepherd's arm. The element of surprise inherent in the Chatsworth version has now disappeared. The four figures are arranged symmetrically on either side of the tomb, a simple rectangular block, conveying a new, calmer rhythm of composition. Panofsky has suggested a change in interpretation: 'The Louvre painting no longer represents the dramatic encounter with

Death, but rather a calm contemplation on the theme of mortality.' 'Ego' no longer bears reference to the skull but to the person buried in this blissful place. Claude Lévi-Strauss recently suggested that, rather than 'invert the meaning of the Latin expression as Panofsky did,' one should see 'in the young girl, standing silently, Death, or in any event, Fate.' In this sense, it is she who utters the *Et in Arcadia Ego*, which the young kneeling shepherd seems to indicate, as he turns to her, pointing to the inscription. Poussin invites us to meditate on the frailty of things human and on the ephemeral quality of human happiness.

This mysterious young woman (perhaps Death) bears no resemblance to the more lightly dressed figure in the Chatsworth version. She 'exemplifies, in a simple rural setting, that presence of the supernatural with which Poussin, by other means, has always known how to imbue his landscapes.' (Lévi-Strauss).

The Dance to the Music of Time

Poussin excelled in the genre of 'moral poetry' as in *The Arcadian Shepherds*. Although far less well known, this painting in the Wallace Collection is nevertheless equally successful, its subject having been chosen, according to Poussin's biographer, Bellori, by Cardinal Giulio Rospigliosi, the future Pope Clement IX. Rospigliosi, a man of letters and a poet was, like Poussin, a member of the erudite Barberini circle.

Time, with his lyre, is playing the tune to which the four allegorical figures dance, one man and three women, whom we can identify as representing the four states through which man passes: poverty, industry, wealth and idle luxury. These four conditions each have an effect on the others: industry transforms poverty into wealth, but idle luxury brings wealth back to poverty. Apollo's chariot crosses the sky, preceded by Aurora and followed by the Hours. With a totally novel approach, Poussin incorporates elements alluding to Vanity: the two putti, one holding an hourglass, the other blowing soap bubbles, emphasize the ephemeral character of all things. Poussin has succeeded in turning this composite whole into a graceful scene, balanced in perfect symmetry, enhanced with light, vivid colours. The date is close to that of the second version of *The Arcadian Shepherds*, around 1638-1640.

*The Dance to the Music of Time, c.*1638-1640. Oil on canvas, 83 x 105 cm.
London, The Wallace Collection.

Landscape with St Matthew and the Angel

Purchased by Gian Maria Roscioli, priest and secretary to Pope Urban VIII, shortly before Poussin's departure for Paris, this *St Matthew*, together with its pendant *St John on Patmos* (Chicago, The Art Institute), heralds the artist's interest in large landscapes, an interest which developed and matured around the 1650s.

St Matthew, inspired by an angel, is seated in the foreground of a vast landscape of ruins and mountains, working on his Gospel. The idea of placing the scene out of doors shows Poussin's ability to create new compositions, rather than follow the pictorial tradition which set the Evangelists in an interior (one thinks, for example, of Caravaggio's paintings of St Matthew). Here St Matthew and the Angel seem to be conversing intimately, the sole living beings in a vast landscape in which can be seen the ruined tower, the Torre delle Milizie, and the river Tiber near the Acqua Acetosa on the approaches to Rome. According to classical symbolism, the New Testament was born on the ruins of the Ancient World.

The German painter and biographer Joachim von Sandrart* speaks of visiting the Roman Campagna in the company of Poussin and Claude Lorrain in order to sketch. The surviving pictorial evidence of these outings is scarce indeed, but Poussin, inspired by reality, has created an ideal and serene image of nature. It was only later that he incorporated people into the backgrounds of his landscapes.

* see bibliography

Oil on canvas, 99 x 135 cm, prior to 1640. Berlin, Staatliche Museen, Gemäldegalerie.

This noble and solitary landscape, in which St Matthew has stopped to work on his Gospel, is strewn with ruins, the symbols of the Ancient World on which the New Testament was built.

The Sacraments

(second series)

Few artists have dared to portray the seven Sacraments in seven separate paintings. Poussin's astonishing *tour de force* is that he painted two complete sequences, very different in treatment. Two years separate the end of one from the beginning of the other. In 1642, in Paris, the artist finished the last painting of the first series, *Baptism* (Washington, National Gallery of Art), destined for Cassiano dal Pozzo. Probably envious, Chantelou asked for copies of these paintings. Cassiano refused and offered him 'coloured drawings' instead. Poussin himself showed little inclination to find a copyist. As with the *Self-Portraits* later on, the artist finally set about the task himself and in March 1644 decided to undertake a second series with an entirely different approach – a result perhaps of his much documented dislike of repetition.

Poussin did not choose scenes from everyday life for his *Sacraments,* but sought to reconstitute the world of the early Church, drawing inspiration from both the life of Christ and that of the Virgin. Thus to evoke *Baptism,* he chose Christ's baptism by St John the Baptist; for *Penance,* the meal at the home of Simon the Pharisee; for *Ordination,* Christ giving the keys to St Peter; and, naturally, for the *Eucharist,* the Last Supper. *Marriage* is based on that of the Virgin; *Confirmation* and *Extreme Unction* are in accordance with the earliest rules laid down by the Church.

Unlike the first series, we have excellent information, from the letters that have been preserved, on the order in which Poussin executed the paintings, and it is consequently possible to date them precisely. We have maintained this order in preference to the one traditionally adopted by the Catholic faith.

In Chantelou's residence, in Paris, the *Sacraments* were hung behind small curtains which the viewer was invited to draw aside one after the other, in order to view the paintings in sequence. In a letter to his friend and patron, Poussin approved of the idea: 'Your intention to veil the paintings is excellent; showing them one by one will ensure that one does not weary of them; seeing them all together would fill the senses too much at one time' (24 May 1648). Bernini's famous remark after seeing the paintings during a visit to Paris in 1665 is worth repeating: after an evening walk and having aired his opinion on a thousand other matters, Bernini turned to his host and said, 'I am unable to rid my mind of those paintings.'

Opposite:
Pen and ink, black chalk, brown wash.
Paris, Louvre, Graphic Arts Department.

Oil on canvas, 117 x 178 cm, 1644.
Edinburgh, Duke of Sutherland Collection, on loan to the National Gallery of Scotland.

Extreme Unction

'Yesterday I began work on one of the Sacraments. *I pray to God that He grants me enough days to finish all seven.*'
(*Letter to Chantelou, 15 April 1644*)

'*I am working with great fervour on the Extreme Unction which, it is true, is a subject worthy of an artist like Apelles (because he greatly enjoyed depicting the dying). […] The said painting will contain seventeen figures of men, women and children, young and old, some of whom are shedding their tears, the others praying to God for the dying man.*'
(*Letter to Chantelou, 25 April 1644*)

79

Confirmation

'Your painting of Confirmation [...] contains twenty-four figures almost all represented full-length, besides the background architecture, and I think that I shall need at least five or six months to finish it; furthermore [Sir] you should bear in mind that these are not works which one can paint whilst whistling like your painters in Paris who will make you a painting in the space of twenty-four hours. I feel I have achieved a lot when I paint one head in a day, so long as I achieve my desired effect.'

(Letter to Chantelou, 20 August 1645)

Oil on canvas, 117 x 178 cm, 1645.
Edinburgh, Duke of Sutherland Collection,
on loan to the National Gallery of Scotland.

Baptism

'If the Baptism which you may have received seems to some people too sweet, I beg them to believe that I am not like those who, when singing, always adopt the same tone and I know how to bring variety when I wish to do so.'

(Letter to Chantelou, 24 March 1647)

Oil on canvas, 117 x 178 cm, 1646.
Edinburgh, Duke of Sutherland Collection,
on loan to the National Gallery of Scotland.

Pen and ink, black chalk, brown wash.
Paris, Louvre, Graphic Arts Department.

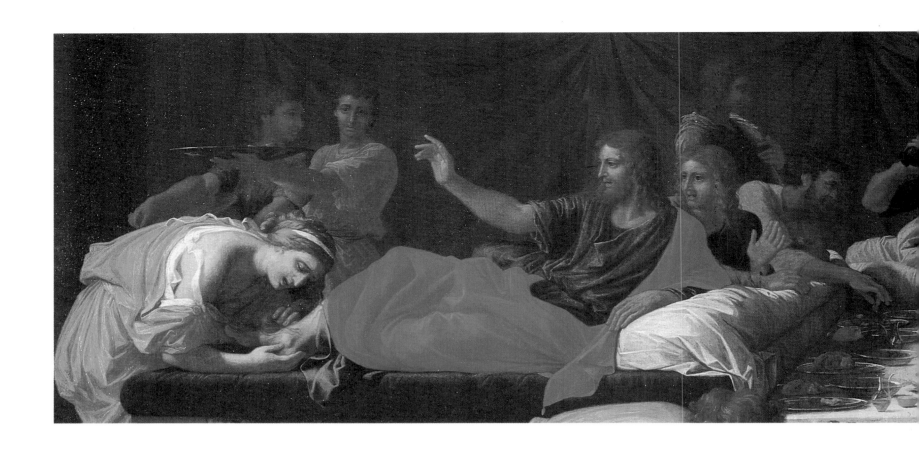

Oil on canvas, 117 x 178 cm, 1646-1647.
Edinburgh, Duke of Sutherland Collection, on loan to the National Gallery of Scotland.

Penance

'I am sending you the Penance which I have finished. I shall give you no introduction, for the subject is depicted in such a way as not to require any interpretation, provided one has read the Gospels.'

(Letter to Chantelou, 3 June 1647)

Oil on canvas, 117 x 178cm, 1647.
Edinburgh, Duke of Sutherland Collection, on loan to the National Gallery of Scotland.

Ordination

'I tell you in all sincerity that I have done for you what I would do for no other living person, and that I shall persist in my resolve to serve you with all my heart. I am neither fickle nor inconstant when I have once pledged my affection.'

(Letter to Chantelou, 24 November 1647)

Oil on canvas, 117 x 178cm, 1647.
Edinburgh, Duke of Sutherland Collection, on loan to the National Gallery of Scotland.

Eucharist

'Nevertheless I have prepared for you a Supper which depicts Him who has shown us how to suffer all things.'

Pen and ink, black chalk, brown wash.
Paris, Louvre, Graphic Arts Department.

Marriage

(Letter to Chantelou, 3 November 1647)

'I have done my utmost and have enriched it with figures. As
you can see, I have taken more than four months to complete
it, with nothing else in mind than how to find the means of
satisfying you.'

(Letter to Chantelou, 23 March 1648)

Oil on canvas, 117 x 178 cm, 1647-1648.
Edinburgh, Duke of Sutherland Collection,
on loan to the National Gallery of Scotland.

Moses trampling on Pharaoh's Crown

The life of Moses inspired Poussin on several occasions. Poussin twice depicted the story of the infant Moses trampling on Pharaoh's crown, of which the second version, now in the Louvre, was painted in 1648. This earlier version was most probably executed in Rome for Jean Pointel, in 1645, three years after Poussin's return from Paris.

Pharaoh and his daughter Thermusis – who has found the baby Moses and brought him out of the Nile – are shown in a highly symmetrical construction in which the figures are arranged as in a frieze. The daughter presents Moses to her father, who playfully places his crown on the child's head. The infant lets it fall and tramples on it, whereupon the High Priest rushes towards him, a dagger in his hand. Once again, Moses is saved through the intervention of Pharaoh's daughter. The child's sacrilegious act, barely visible in the painting, provokes surprise, anxiety, indignation and apprehension amongst the onlookers. Neither the setting, which consists only of a few architectural elements and a palm tree, nor the minute detail with which Poussin paints the Pharaoh's couch and the stool on which his daughter is seated, can distract from the dramatic episode. The magnificent drapery and expanses of colour give movement to the scene.

Oil on canvas, 99 x 142 cm, 1645.
Woburn (Bedfordshire), Woburn Abbey.

Eliezer and Rebecca

Conceived as a relaxation after the completion of the austere, second series of *Sacraments*, this painting is a masterpiece of grace and innovation. Painted in 1648 for Jean Pointel, Poussin's principal French patron alongside Chantelou, it was bought by the duc de Richelieu, and in 1665, when the collection was dispersed, it passed into royal ownership.

As Félibien remarked, Poussin seems to be more preoccupied with describing 'a number of young women embodying different kinds of beauty' than with illustrating the passage from the *Genesis* (24, 13-14), in which Eliezer, Abraham's servant sent off to Mesopotamia with the delicate mission of finding a wife for Isaac, his master's son, and then bringing her back to the land of the Canaanites, stops at a well outside the town of Nachor at a time when 'the daughters of the men of the city come out to draw water.' Guided by God towards the young girl who gives him and his camels water to quench their thirst, he gives her 'a golden earring [...], and two (gold) bracelets for her hands' (one can see them in his left hand), in the knowledge that she is the one destined for Isaac. A multitude of expressions and emotions fill the faces of the young women surrounding Eliezer and Rebecca: reproachful (that of the young girl leaning on the amphora),

delighted – or annoyed – (the two young women on the extreme right), curious and intrigued (that of the young girl emptying the contents of her pitcher into that of her companion) or totally indifferent to the scene (the small group on the left or the young girl preoccupied with lifting a container out of the well). Each stands out against the background of a beautiful landscape of deep, elongated shadows and a geometrical arrangement of the architecture.

In a famous lecture on the painting delivered at the Paris Academy, Philippe de Champaigne (1602–74) solemnly reproached the artist for not having 'treated the subject of his painting with complete fidelity to the story, since he had omitted the camels which are explicitly mentioned in the Bible.' Surely every modern viewer agrees with Le Brun, Louis XIV's principal court painter, who justified this omission as follows: in order to make a scene seem pleasant, Poussin eliminated 'all the strange things which might lead the eye of the viewer astray' in order to give full weight to 'poetry.' The poetry here lies in the encounter, brought about by divine intervention, between Abraham's aged servant and the beautiful young girl who, shy and modest though she may be, is aware of the destiny which lies before her.

Oil on canvas, 118 x 197 cm, 1648. Paris, Louvre.

Overleaf:

This charming scene, portrayed with such apparent spontaneity, is in reality contained within a complex geometrical framework. The key lies in the subtle visual relationship between the rounded forms of the water jars and the sphere atop the truncated column to the right of the painting. The main lines of the composition, originating from the sphere, are indicated by the placing of the jars. Typically, the interplay between structure and incident reflects Poussin's lifelong theme – the elevation of reason over emotion.

Landscape with the Ashes of Phocion

The painting has as its pendant *Landscape with the Body of Phocion carried out of Athens* (Cardiff, National Museum of Wales). In all likelihood, both were painted in 1648 for Serisier, a Lyon silk merchant, one of the first to collect Poussin's paintings during the seventeenth century. The artist most probably drew his inspiration from Plutarch's *Life of Phocion,* at the end of which the two episodes depicted are evoked in succession. Phocion, an outstanding Athenian general and statesman of the fourth century BC, was summarily sentenced to death by an assembly of the people for political errors, and was made to drink hemlock. His body was banned from Attica and a decree was passed, forbidding the lighting of a pyre for his funeral rites. Canopion, a poor man, carried the body out of Athens to the neighbouring state of Megara (the subject of the Cardiff painting). There the general's remains were burned and a 'Megarite woman', accompanied by her servant, collected the ashes and carried them back to Athens, hoping to shame the Athenians into recognizing their mistake. Shortly afterwards, the penitent Athenians decreed a public burial for Phocion's ashes and erected a statue in his honour.

Although set in the foreground, the two women remain in semi-darkness as they pay their final respects to the general amid a noble, symmetrical landscape in which the city of Megara and lush vegetation seem more important than the narrative event itself.

In 1665, when he was living in Paris, Bernini saw this painting and, striking his forehead, immediately exclaimed: 'Monsieur Poussin is a painter who works from here.' The overwhelming impression is of the contrast between the vast, majestic portrayal of the landscape, dominated by verdant nature, and the small scale accorded to human figures and events.

*Landscape with the
Ashes of Phocion*, 1648.
Oil on canvas,
116 x 176cm.
Liverpool, Walker
Art Gallery, National
Museums &
Galleries on
Merseyside.

101

The Judgment of Solomon

The Judgment of Solomon was painted in 1649 for Jean Pointel. According to Bellori, Poussin considered it to be his best work. The story, drawn from the Old Testament (*Kings,* III, 16-28), concerns two prostitutes, each of whom had a child. One of them has suffocated hers during its sleep and secretly exchanged it for the child of the other woman – who soon realized what had happened. The two women came before Solomon in order for justice to be done. As they quarrelled, the king announced his decision: 'Divide the living child in two and give half to one, half to the other.' The reactions of the two women are diametrically opposed: the first begs for mercy: 'O my Lord, give her the living child and in no wise slay it'; the other simply says: 'Let it be neither mine nor thine, but divide it.' Upon hearing these words, Solomon recognizes the real mother who pleaded for

mercy and says, 'Give her the living child and in no wise slay it: she is the mother.' If we accept that the wicked mother, green with anger, is on the right, it is difficult to comprehend why she should be holding her dead child. The good mother, petrified with horror, holds open her arms as she utters 'do not slay it', whilst the young judge Solomon, isolated upon his throne, is simultaneously giving the order and sentence as he points towards the good mother to whom the child rightfully belongs. The triangle formed by the three central figures does not prevent us from noticing the soldier, whose duty it is to execute the king's orders. The motif of the still, facing griffins on the base of the throne echoes the violent confrontation between the two women. Both the audacity of Poussin's use of colour and the force of his narrative expression are equally to be admired.

Oil on canvas, 101 x 150 cm, 1649. Paris, Louvre.

In his Notes on Painting, *collected and passed down to us by Bellori, Poussin speaks of his fascinated and urgent concern for 'the shape of things': 'Colours in a painting are like decoys which seduce the eye — like beautiful lines in a poem.'*

The Ecstasy of St Paul

'He aspires, in his own twisted way, to make me laugh; but on the contrary I ought to weep,' Poussin declared in a letter dated 12 January 1648, with regard to *Typhon*, a burlesque verse epic, which the great French poet, Paul Scarron, had sent to him (Scarron wished to have a painting by the artist). After twice refusing, first in 1646 and then in 1648, Poussin finally agreed to paint a bacchanal, changing it at the last minute, not without a certain mischievousness, to the *Ecstasy of St Paul,* thereby alluding to Scarron's patron saint.

Once again, Poussin has treated the theme with great originality. He stages the scene in an architectural frame flanked on the left by a pier and on the right by a wall. The perspective of the architecture directs the eye to the landscape beyond, which is probably like the countryside which Poussin had observed in the Roman Campagna. Below the saint, Poussin has painted his traditional symbols, as if in a separate still-life. Paul is held up by three angels forming a compact group of figures, whose hands and feet seem to move with balletic grace and energy. A masterpiece of rhythm and coherence, this composition is exceptional for its chromatic subtleties and for the delicate golden light which is so harmoniously dispersed over the canvas.

Oil on canvas, 148 x 120 cm, 1649-1650.
Paris, Louvre.

The Self-Portraits

Poussin's correspondence with his patrons gives us fairly precise information as to the circumstances under which these two *Self-Portraits* were executed. As early as 1647, Paul Fréart de Chantelou, at much the same time as Jean Pointel, wished to have a portrait of the artist. In the first instance, Poussin tried evading the issue by finding another artist of good repute in the art of portraiture, a field in which 'he took no great pleasure and had little experience'. Had he not been faced with these repeated requests from his two patrons, and with the impossibility of finding a painter capable of portraying him according to his taste, Poussin would probably have never depicted himself. He finally set to work in 1649: the first painting, originally destined to go to Chantelou, was finished on 20 June 1649. But before sending it off, he wrote to his friend: 'I have done one of my portraits and soon I shall start on the other. I will send you the one which I have executed better, but please, you must not breathe a word of it, so as to avoid any jealousy.' The second portrait was finished in May 1650, but Poussin changed the two *Self-Portraits* around: Chantelou was to have the most recent since, according to the painter, it was 'the better painting with the better likeness.' We note the skill with which he has played upon the rivalry of his two patrons.

Within the space of only a few months, Poussin has portrayed himself in quite different fashions, varying both the composition and his approach. The Berlin portrait, the less famous of the two, seems to have suffered from the artist's own aesthetic judgment; he presents himself drawing (in his left hand is a drawing pencil) and he is resting his right hand on a book, which appears to be a large drawing pad. His face, in three-quarter view, stands out against the rectangular slab of stone framed by a garland of laurel leaves carried by two putti. The Latin inscription gives the date when the work was executed as well as the age, origins and qualifications of the model. The overall, rather austere impression, emphasized by the large black cloak which can also be seen in the Louvre portrait, is softened by the slight smile on the model's face.

In the second portrait, Poussin no longer places the emphasis on references to classical antiquity but rather on painting itself. Sterner and more solemn, the painter, resting his right hand on a portfolio, is standing in front of paintings stacked against the wall, one of which is turned around and contains a Latin inscription, briefer this time, stating only his name, age and place of birth. On a large canvas jutting out from behind, a half-length portrait can be seen, that of a woman

Oil on canvas, 78 x 65cm, 1649.
Berlin, Staatliche Museen, Gemäldegalerie.

NICOLAVS POVSSINVS ANDELYENSIS ACADEMICVS ROMANVS PRIMVS
PICTOR ORDINARIVS LVDOVICI IVSTI REGIS GALLIÆ. ANNO Domini
1649. Roma.   ÆTATIS SVÆ.55.

wearing a diadem with an eye in it and held by two arms reaching out to her. Already in the seventeenth century, the Italian biographer, Bellori, had given the key to this allegory: 'The head of the woman in profile with an eye at the top of her diadem symbolizes Painting; the two hands which appear and enfold her represent both the Lover of this symbol of Painting and Friendship to whom the painting pays tribute.' For Chantelou, his main French patron, who owned no less than eleven of his canvases and for whom the artist had just finished the second series of *Sacraments,* Poussin positions his portrait within the double metaphor of Painting and Friendship which symbolically united the two men: the artist and his patron.

Bellori, Poussin's Italian biographer and contem-porary, has left us a beautiful verbal portrait of the artist: 'He was tall in stature, well formed and graced with a most rare temperament; his skin had an olive sheen and his hair was black though largely whitened by age. His eyes were as blue as the sky ; his finely chiselled nose and broad forehead brought nobility to the modesty of his face. He was seemly of his person, his garments were not splendid but severe, and they did him honour.'

Oil on canvas, 98 x 74 cm, 1650.
Paris, Louvre.

Landscape with a Storm

In 1651, the same year as the *Landscape with Pyramus and Thisbe* (see page 112), Poussin executed another landscape for Jean Pointel based on the storm theme, with a work depicting a landscape in calm weather. The two paintings, recently rediscovered, form an important addition to Poussin's work as a landscape artist, perhaps still the least well-known aspect of his art. The *Landscape with Tree Struck by Lightning,* known as the *Storm,* is described in an anecdotal fashion in Pointel's inventory as '...a thunderstorm with a cart pulled by oxen.' Although a less immediately interesting subject than the tragic story of the two mythological heroes in the *Landscape with Pyramus and Thisbe,* this representation of a storm is undoubtedly innovative. The painting was greatly admired by Poussin's contemporaries. Félibien wrote a powerful response as if he were himself within the painting: 'Whilst on one side we were watching the storm cloud burst open, admiring the varying effects of the lightning-bolts upon that part of the land all drowned in obscurity, and wondering at the manner in which, during these moments, the figures were illuminated, we saw the sky suddenly change, the clouds gathering in from all parts, veiling it in no time at all. A howling wind was blowing, creating whirlwinds of dust which darkened the air such that one could scarcely see either sky or land. [...] The tallest trees bending before the violence of the gale were bowing their heads as far as the ground; and one could hear those which most resisted split and crack open with a great noise.' In his other works, Poussin often shows human passions and events measured and distanced against the scale and power of nature. Here nature itself, uncontrollable and sovereign, leaves its mark on human destiny with overwhelming strength.

Oil on canvas, 99 x 132 cm, 1651.
Rouen, Musée des Beaux-Arts.

Landscape with Pyramus and Thisbe

According to Félibien, the painting was executed for Poussin's lifelong friend, Cassiano dal Pozzo. Félibien quotes from a letter (now lost) from the artist to the painter Jacques Stella, explaining what he had endeavoured to achieve: 'I have tried to depict a storm over the land [...]. All the figures that can be seen, play their part in relation to the weather; some flee through the dust and are carried along by the wind; others, on the contrary, battle against the wind and walk with difficulty, putting their hands before their eyes. [...] In the foreground of the picture, you see Pyramus, stretched out dead on the ground, and beside him, Thisbe, giving way to her grief.'

This is a love story which begins like a fairytale and ends in a double suicide. Night having fallen, Thisbe the Babylonian awaits her lover Pyramus under a mulberry tree. A wild lioness, having just attacked some oxen, continues to roam around the area. Thisbe runs to take refuge in a cave but in her hurry loses a veil which the lioness shreds to pieces with her bloodstained mouth. Pyramus arrives shortly afterwards and discovers the veil. Believing her to have been devoured, he stabs himself in the side in despair. Thisbe returns and, faced with the sight of such horror, inflicts the same fate upon herself with the wish that the mulberry tree should forever recall the blood which had been shed, and bear 'dark fruit fitted for sorrow.'

Once again, Poussin illustrates how destiny is driven by a series of accidents and misunderstandings, by 'those tricks of Fate', as he called them. The painting is composed of a number of scenes which make up the background: a lion attacking herdsmen on horseback, forcing a shepherd to flee and abandon his flock, a dog, its coat bristling, watching without daring to come near. Thunder and lightning strike, here on a tree trunk, there on a building on top of the hill. The remarkable result of this 'storm on land,' as Poussin so perfectly described it, demonstrates how human tragedies can only be compared with the awesome forces of nature.

Oil on canvas, 192 x 273 cm, 1651.
Frankfurt, Städelsches Kunstinstitut.

The Death of Sapphira

During the last ten years of his life, Poussin did not confine himself totally to painting landscapes, but also turned his attention towards the representation of townscapes. The unyielding austerity of the architecture, which accompanies and rigorously frames the composition, perfectly complements the subject-matter. Drawn from *Acts of the Apostles* (V, 1-11), *The Death of Sapphira* focuses on a period of the early Christian communities which had been founded by Peter and Paul. Ananias and his wife, Sapphira, had sold a piece of land and lied about the sum received, secretly keeping a portion of the money which they were supposed to hand over to the Apostles. Reproached by Peter for un-Christian selfishness, both were struck down by Divine Justice, one after the other. The Apostles, standing on the finely paved steps, are pointing at the sky and towards Anania, taking on the appearance of avenging deities. The clear light picks out a fortress built on a craggy outcrop overlooking the town, in which some scholars recognize certain Roman palaces or a recollection of Château-Gaillard which dominates Poussin's birthplace, Les Andelys. The severity of the construction, together with the brilliance of the use of colour, should not, however, be allowed to overshadow the reference made to charity, as indicated by the group so centrally set in the middle distance.

Oil on canvas, 122 x 199 cm, 1652. Paris, Louvre.

The Exposing of Moses

Painters have been more inclined to tackle the theme of Moses being saved by the Pharaoh's daughter than that of Moses being exposed on the water (*Exodus*, 2, 1-22). In order to protect his throne, Pharaoh had ordered that 'Every son that is born ye shall cast into the river.' In order to save him, Moses' mother, after having hidden him for three months, 'took for him an ark of bulrushes [...] and she laid it in the flags by the river's brink'. In the painting, she looks round anxiously at her worried husband, who turns away in pain. Miriam, who is keeping watch, points towards a group of women in the distance, probably Pharaoh's daughter and her attendants. Poussin makes references to Egypt by painting a sphinx with a female head (whose reflection in the river Nile can be seen in the foreground). Beside the sphinx reclines the personification of the fruitful river Nile, bedecked with flowers, who reaches out a protective arm. However, the landscape draws its inspiration from Roman monuments: the Castel sant' Angelo and the Temple of Vesta at Tivoli. As for the building whose roof is shaped like a pyramid, it was inspired by an architectural engraving in a book by Pirro Ligorio. Carried out for Jacques Stella in 1654, the painting marks a distinct change of style in Poussin's art: despite the diagonals formed by their gazes, the figures seem to be very much isolated.

Oil on canvas,
150 x 204 cm, 1654.
Oxford, Ashmolean Museum.

Landscape with Orion

Painted in 1658 for Michel Passart, *auditeur* and then *maître des Comptes* in Paris, this intensely complex, haunting work drew its inspiration from a number of sources identified by Gombrich, amongst them Lucian, Ovid, Cartari and Natale Conti. The giant Orion is seeking his way to the sun whose rays would heal him of his blindness, which is the punishment inflicted upon him by King Oenopion after his attempt to rape Queen Aerope. Guided by Cedalion who is perched upon his shoulders and Hephaestus who stands at his feet, Orion is walking towards the sun which is hidden by the clouds. Orion had three fathers: Jupiter, Apollo and Neptune, respectively representing the Air, the Sun and Water, all three elements being essential to cloud formation, and more generically to all forms of life. According to Homer, the hunting goddess Diana, who is leaning on a cloud high up in the sky, was in love with Orion (who was a hunter, hence the bow and quiver which he carries), and so is here represented as watching over him.

Over and beyond the message contained in the painting (Orion as victim of his desires), there is the extraordinary invention, unique in the seventeenth century, of this giant whom we know to be in communion with Nature and whose monumental and mysterious grandeur he shares.

Oil on canvas, 119 x 183 cm, 1658. New York, Metropolitan Museum of Art.

The Four Seasons

The Four Seasons are, as is often said, Poussin's 'spiritual and artistic testament'. At the age of sixty four, the old and suffering artist accepted a commission from the duc de Richelieu, to undertake this ultimate creation which would last four years, from 1660–1664.

Rather than represent the *Seasons* through conventional allegorical heads of figures and their various attributes, Poussin chose to give the cyclical seasons specific episodes drawn from the Old Testament, hence conferring upon each painting a Biblical basis.

Spring represents the Garden of Eden (*Genesis*, 2). Adam and Eve are seated amidst lush vegetation before the Fall. But Eve is already pointing her finger towards the Tree of Knowledge.

Summer draws its source from the *Book of Ruth.* Having only just arrived in Bethlehem, the young Moabite asks Boaz's permission to glean in his fields. In turn Boaz questions his servant as to the identity of this young woman to whom he is offering his protection. Touched by the young woman's choice to leave her native land and adopt

that of '[...] the Lord God of Israel, under whose wings (she hath) come to trust' (*Ruth*, 2, 12), he then takes her to be his wife.

Autumn overflows with nature's generosity, beautifully suggested by the enormous bunch of grapes which has been carried back from the Promised Land by Moses' messengers (*Numbers*, 13). One of the men carries pomegranates, the young woman seen from behind is also holding a basket of fruit, whilst another figure, perched on a ladder, is picking apples.

Winter represents the scene of the Flood taken from Genesis (*Genesis* 8). Exasperated by the selfishness of all men, Jehovah decides to 'strike them from the face of the earth,' with the sole exception of Noah and his family who took refuge in the Ark, visible on the left in the distance. It then rained for forty days and forty nights. In contrast to Michelangelo's ceiling in the Sistine Chapel, Poussin's work does not represent a mass of men and women desperately trying to save their lives. Instead, through a few unforgettable images, he expresses all the despair of the situation: a man

The tremulous quality of the artist's late work, luminous with colour, was to influence Cézanne, a great admirer of Poussin: 'Imagine that Poussin had devoted himself entirely to landscape – that for me is classical art.'

(Cézanne, letter to Joachim Gasquet, 1926)

Spring (detail).

Summer (detail).

Autumn (detail).

Winter (detail).

Spring

letting go of his horse's ears, another gripping a plank of wood, a child being hoisted up onto a rock by his mother, a last prayer to heaven ... All in all, a tableau of final, hopeless moments before total destruction, the end of the world. The snake alone is a spectator of this scene of despair, but it is also a symbol of rebirth, perhaps heralding the Resurrection.

From *Spring* to *Winter*, we travel through the book of Life from birth to death. But Poussin was also representing the four times of the day, from sunrise to nightfall, striving to capture with accuracy the subtle variations of light through a range of tonalities: green for *Spring*, pale yellow for *Summer*, yellow ochre for *Autumn* and greyish green, almost monochrome, for *Winter*.

By virtue of its richness and scope, this cycle has given rise to many scholarly interpretations and commentaries. Central to all, however, there stands the ageing artist's final judgement on the destiny of mankind. Chateaubriand's celebrated phrase, taken from *La Vie de Rancé* defines the powerful emotion engendered by this final masterpiece: 'This painting communicates the increasing isolation of age and the trembling hand of an old man – but what a marvellous trembling time has wrought! Genius often heralds the approaching end with a masterpiece: a final flurry of wings as the soul takes flight.'

Oil on canvas, 117 x 160 cm, 1660-1664.
Paris, Louvre.

Summer

Oil on canvas,
117 x 160cm, 1660-1664.
Paris, Louvre.

Autumn

Oil on canvas, 117 x 160 cm,
1660-1664.
Paris, Louvre.

Winter

Oil on canvas, 117 x 160 cm,
1660-1664.
Paris, Louvre.

Spring (detail).

Summer (detail).

Autumn (detail).

Winter (detail).

Select biography

1594 (June) Birth of Nicolas Poussin in Les Andelys in Normandy, probably in the hamlet of Villiers. The registers of baptism into the Roman Catholic Church during the years 1593 and 1594 have disappeared, so there is no actual record of Poussin's baptism, nor a more precise date of birth. According to his French biographer, Félibien, the painter's father, Jean Poussin, 'came from Soissons and those who knew him swear he was of a noble family, but that his fortune was small.' His mother, Marie de Laisement, was the widow of a minor legal officer of Vernon. Jean Poussin had sided with the Protestant Henri de Navarre against the Catholic League, and served as a soldier. Still according to Félibien, he had taken part in the storming of Vernon alongside one of his uncles, after which he married Marie de Laisement and, according to Passeri, settled in Les Andelys in 1592.

1594-1612 According to his biographers, Poussin was given a solid education and seemed keen on his studies, but his 'penchant for drawing' (Félibien), from which no one could dissuade him finally gained the upper hand. The painter Quentin Varin (c.1570-1634), who is regarded as Poussin's first master, lived in Les Andelys between 1611-12, and appears to have encouraged the young boy's vocation.

1612-1621 At the age of 18, Poussin quietly leaves the family home and makes his way to Paris. There he works in the studios of two artists; studying first under Georges Lallemant (c.1575-1636) and then under Ferdinand Elle (c.1580-1649). Both apprenticeships are brief and of little consequence. He also studies and copies engravings by Raphael and Giulio Romano. He then meets a rich young gentleman who invites him to the Poitou region to paint in his castle, but the scheme is soon abandoned. His biographers maintain that on his journey back to Paris he executed two paintings for the Capuchin church at Blois and some *Bacchanals* for the castle of Cheverny; there is, however, no documentary proof. On his way back to the capital he falls ill from exhaustion and returns to Les Andelys, where he spends a year recovering his health. He then returns to Paris and attempts his first journey to Rome, but gets no further than Florence. A second attempted journey ends in Lyon.

1622 For the celebrations organized by the Jesuits in Paris following the canonization of their saints, Ignatius Loyola and Francis Xavier, Poussin is commissioned to paint six paintings, now lost, which he executes in the space of six days. The well-known poet, Giambattista Marino (1569-1625), living in Paris at the time, takes an interest in Poussin. The young artist does drawings for him, most of which illustrate episodes taken from Ovid's *Metamorphoses* (Windsor, Royal Collection). He also executes a few decorative panels for the palace of Marie de Médicis at the Luxembourg, and a painting for Notre-Dame, *The Death of the Virgin*, now lost.

1623-1624   Encouraged by Marino who had left Paris the year before, Poussin leaves Paris for Italy, making a short stay in Venice (according to another of his biographers, Mancini), before reaching Rome in the spring of 1624. There he meets up with the poet, who introduces him to Marcello Sacchetti (1586-1629), the papal secretary and an active patron of the arts, who 'won for him the favour of Cardinal Francesco Barberini, nephew of Pope Urban VIII' (Félibien). Poussin is thirty years old and these early years in Rome are times of hardship. Whilst studying from the Antique he also copies Titian, notably his *Bacchanal of the Andrians* (Madrid, Museo del Prado).

1626-1627   Poussin moves to the Via Paolina, sharing a house with the Flemish sculptor François Duquesnoy (1594-1643). Together they measure and draw sculptures from classical antiquity. He receives a major commission from Cardinal Francesco Barberini (1597-1679), *The Death of Germanicus* (Minneapolis, The Minneapolis Institute of Arts). Félibien mentions the painter's admiration for Domenichino. He copies his *St Andrew Led to Martyrdom* (Rome, San Gregorio al Monte) and frequents his school where he is able to draw from life models.

1628-1629   Poussin executes his first recorded public commission, for St Peter's: *The Martyrdom of St Erasmus* (Rome, Vatican Museums), his earliest extant altarpiece.

1629-1630   He executes other paintings with similarly large scale figures, *The Virgin appearing to St James* and *The Inspiration of the Poet* (both Paris, Louvre).
Poussin is ill and for a number of years suffers from the 'mal di Francia', most probably syphilis. He recovers in 1630 through the care of a French cook, Jacques Dughet, whose daughter, Anne-Marie, he marries on 9th September 1630 in his parish church of San Lorenzo in Lucina. Nevertheless, it seems that the artist was later to suffer from after-effects of the illness, which probably caused the trembling of his hands, which he begins to complain of as early as 1642.

1631   The couple live with Anne-Marie's brother, Gaspard Dughet (1615-1675). Poussin is elected member of the Academy of St Luke, and Cassiano dal Pozzo (1588-1657) becomes his principal patron. The times of hardship are over.
He gives evidence at the trial of Fabrizio Valguarnera, accused of smuggling diamonds and paintings. A number of Poussin's works are mentioned in the deposition, amongst which *The Plague* (Paris, Louvre) and *The Kingdom of Flora* (Dresden, Staatliche Kunstsammlungen).

1632   Poussin settles in the Via Paolina, still with his brother-in-law, Gaspard Dughet, who is later to become a landscape artist. Poussin strengthens his ties with the archeological circles of Rome, notably those surrounding Cassiano dal Pozzo and his Museo Cartaceo (Paper Museum), a vast accumulation of drawings depicting ancient works of art which Poussin must have known and to whose elaboration he probably contributed. Today, the drawings can be found at Windsor Castle, the British Museum and in a number of private collections. Poussin also works on Leonardo da Vinci's *Treatise* (then in Cardinal Barberini's library) which he illustrates.

1635 Cardinal Richelieu (1585-1642) commissions two *Bacchanals* from him which he finishes in 1636. (Whether or not the *Triumph of Venus* in Philadelphia belongs to this series still remains a subject of heated discussion amongst art historians.)

1636 Poussin begins work on his first series of *Sacraments* for Cassiano dal Pozzo (Grantham, Belvoir Castle and Washington, National Gallery of Art).

1639 Early in the year, Poussin receives an official invitation from Richelieu and Sublet de Noyers, his chief adviser in artistic matters, to come to Paris and work for the king. Amongst all the excuses he gives to justify remaining in Rome, Poussin gives as pretext a number of unfinished paintings, amongst them *The Gathering of Manna*, commissioned by Chantelou, major domo to the king who was to be one of Poussin's main French patrons.

1640 Having succeeded in postponing the journey to Paris for over a year and a half, Poussin finally leaves for France on 28th October, in the company of his brother-in-law, Jean Dughet, Paul Chantelou and his brother Roland de Chambray.

1640-1642 Poussin is named first painter in residence to the king, Louis XIII, who commissions from him two altarpieces, one of which is *The Institution of the Eucharist* (Paris, Louvre). The other will never be executed. For Richelieu, he paints *Moses and the Burning Bush* (Copenhagen, Statens Museum for Kunst) and a huge allegorical painting, *Time saving Truth from Envy and Discord* (Paris, Louvre). However, his principal commission is the preparation of designs for the decoration of the Grande Galerie, on the theme of the *Life of Hercules*, for which only a few drawings survive today. By 1642, faced with the pressure of intrigues, demands and rivalries, Poussin has no thought other than that of leaving Paris as soon as possible and returning to Rome. He manages to make his way back at the end of September 1642.

1643 The death of Louis XIII and the disgrace of Sublet de Noyers free Poussin from his responsibilities for the Grande Galerie, whose renovation was under the direction of Rémy Vuibert (*c.*1600-1652) and Jean Lemaire (1598-1659).

1644 The death of Pope Urban VIII brings about a considerable change in the nature of Roman patronage, which had hitherto been extremely francophile. The artist begins his second series of *Sacraments* for Chantelou (Edinburgh, National Gallery of Scotland) and serves as intermediary in the purchasing of 'antique busts'. By the end of the year he has already finished the *Extreme Unchion*.

1645-1648 Poussin begins work on the *Crucifixion* (Hartford, The Wadsworth Atheneum). Whilst completing the second series of *Sacraments*, he turns more and more frequently to painting landscapes: hence the paintings of *Phocion* (Liverpool, Walker Art Gallery and Cardiff, National Museum of Wales), *Diogenes* (Paris, Louvre) and *Landscape with a Man killed by a Snake* (London, National Gallery).

1649   Poussin paints *The Judgment of Solomon* (Paris, Louvre), as well as one *Self Portrait* (Berlin, Staatliche Museen, Gemäldegalerie), for the financier Jean Pointel.

1650   He executes his second *Self-Portrait* (Paris, Louvre) for Chantelou.

1651   Poussin paints the *Landscape with Pyramus and Thisbe* (Frankfurt, Städelisches Kunstinstitut) for Cassiano dal Pozzo, as well as the *Storm* (Rouen, Musée des Beaux-Arts) and *Calm* (Sudeley Castle) for Pointel.

1652   Poussin is unwell and paints little.

1653   He executes *Christ and the Woman Taken in Adultery* (Paris, Louvre) for Le Nôtre, Louis XIV's landscape gardener.

1655   The Abbé Louis Fouquet, in a letter from Rome to his brother Nicolas Fouquet (1615-1680), certifies that Poussin 'works better and more truly than ever before.' His paintings are of a 'surprisingly high cost.' At the request of Nicolas Fouquet Poussin executes, for the castle of Vaux, models of terms which today are at Versailles.

1656   He paints *Achilles Among the Daughters of Lycomedes* (Richmond, Virginia Museum of Fine Arts) for Charles III de Créqui (1624-1687).

1657   Cassiano dal Pozzo dies. It is possible that Poussin executed the *Annunciation* (London, National Gallery) for his tomb. Poussin declines the title of Prince at the Academy of St Luke and paints *The Birth of Bacchus* (Cambridge, Fogg Art Museum) for his friend, the painter Jacques Stella (1596-1657).

1658-1660   Poussin's health is deteriorating but nonetheless he is still 'determined to give of his utmost' (Félibien).

1660-1664   Poussin undertakes the *Four Seasons* for the duc de Richelieu. An extremely moving letter written by Poussin, dated 28th July 1663, shows that the artist was aware of his imminent death: 'I have laid aside my brushes forever, and my only thoughts are of dying which will be the sole cure for the ills which afflict me.' On 14th October 1664, Poussin's wife dies after nine months of illness. *Apollo and Daphne* (Paris, Louvre) is abandoned and given in its unfinished form to Cardinal Camillo Massimi (1620-1677).

1665   In March 1665, six months before his death, Poussin writes a letter to Roland Fréart de Chambray which lays down his artistic creed over the final years and discusses his painting, for which 'the aim is delectation.'
On 19th November, Poussin dies, and is buried in his parish church of San Lorenzo in Lucina, after a solemn but simple funeral.

Index of the principal names cited

General bibliography

BADT K., *Die Kunst des Nicolas Poussin*, 2 vol., Cologne, 1969.

BELLORI G. P., *Le vite de' pittori, scultori ed architetti moderni*, *Rome*, 1672, ed. E. Borea and prefaced by G. Previtali, Torino, 1976.

BIMBENET-PRIVAT M. – THUILLIER J., *La Jeunesse de Poussin: deux documents inconnus*, in course of publicartion.

BLUNT A., *Lettres et propos sur l'Art*, textes réunis et présentés par A. Blunt, Paris, 1964 (rééd., Paris, 1989).

BLUNT A., *The Paintings of Nicolas Poussin. A Critical Catalogue*, 2 vol., London, 1966.

BLUNT A., *Nicolas Poussin. The A.W. Mellon Lectures in the Fine Arts 1958*, *National Gallery of Art, Washington D.C.*, 2 vol., New York-London, 1967.

BLUNT A., *The Drawings of Poussin*, New-Haven, London, 1979.

CHANTELOU P. FRÉART de, *Journal de voyage du Cavalier Bernin en France*, ed. L. Lalanne, Paris, 1885; revised ed., Paris, 1981.

Colloque Nicolas Poussin, sous la direction d'André Chastel (Paris, 1958), 2 vol., Paris, 1960.

DU BOS abbé J.-B., *Réflexions critiques sur la poésie et sur la peinture*, Paris, 1719 (reprint 1993, with preface by Dominique Désirat).

FÉLIBIEN A., *Entretiens sur les vies et sur les ouvrages des plus excellens peintres anciens et modernes*, 5 vol., Paris, 1666-1688; *Nicolas Poussin, 8e Entretien*, IV, Paris, 1685; ed. 1725; ed. Pace, 1981.

FUMAROLI M., 1989, see exh. cat. Paris.

GOMBRICH E. H., "The Subject of Poussin's Orion", *The Burlington Magazine*, LXXXIV, 491, feb 1944, p.37-41 (republished in 1972 in *Symbolic Images Studies in the Art of the Renaissance*, p.119-122.)

JOUANNY Ch., *Correspondance de Nicolas Poussin*, Paris, 1911.

LÉVI-STRAUSS Cl., "En regardant Poussin", *Regarder, Écouter, Lire*, Paris, 1993, p.9-40.

MAHON D., "Poussin's Development: Questions of Method", *The Burlington Magazine*, CII, 691, October 1960, p.455-456

MANCINI G. C., *Considerazioni sulla pittura*, 2 vol., ed. 1956-1957 by A. Marucchi and introduction by L. Salerno.

MÉROT A., *Nicolas Poussin*, Paris, 1990 (American ed., New York, 1990).

PANOFSKY E., "Et in Arcadia Ego. On the Conception of Transience in Poussin and Watteau", *Philosophy and History. Essays presented to E. Cassirer*, Oxford, 1936, p.223-254 new edition with a noticeably different text, under the title of "Et in Arcadia Ego: Poussin and the Elegiac Tradition", *Meaning in the Visual Arts*, Garden City, N.Y., 1955, p.295-320.

ROSENBERG P. - BUTOR N., 1973, see exh. cat. Paris, Louvre.

ROSENBERG P., 1977-1978, see exh. cat. Rome.

ROSENBERG P., 1978, see exh. cat. Dusseldorf.

ROSENBERG P., 1982, see exh. cat. Paris-New York-Chicago.

SANDRART J. von, *Teutsche Academie der edeln Bau, Bild und Mahlerey-Künste*, Nuremberg, 1675; ed. Peltzer, Munich, 1925.

SPARTI D.L., *Le collezioni dal Pozzo. Storia di una famiglia e del suo museo nella Roma seicentesca*, Modena, 1992.

SPARTI D.L., "Appunti sulle finanze di Nicolas Poussin", *Storia dell'Arte*, 79, 1993, p.341-350.

STEEFEL L.D. Jr., "A Neglected Shadow in Poussin's Et in Arcadia Ego", *The Art Bulletin*, CVII, 1, March 1975, p.99-101.

THUILLIER J., *Nicolas Poussin*, Novara, 1969.

THUILLIER J., *Tout l'œuvre peint de Poussin*, Paris, 1974 (Italian ed. Milan, 1974), reed. extended and corrected, 1994.

THUILLIER J., "Poussin et le paysage tragique. 'L'Orage Pointel' au musée des Beaux-Arts de Rouen", *La Revue du Louvre et des Musées de France*, XXVI, 5-6, 1976, p.345-355.

THUILLIER J., *Nicolas Poussin*, Paris, 1988.

WILD D., *Nicolas Poussin*, 2 vol., Zurich, 1980.

WRIGHT C., *Poussin Paintings. A Catalogue Raisonné*, London, 1985; German ed., Landshut, 1989.

Exhibition catalogues

1973: Paris, Musée du Louvre
La Mort de Germanicus (cat. by P. Rosenberg and N. Butor)

1977-1978: Rome, Villa Medici
Nicolas Poussin 1594-1665 (cat. by P. Rosenberg)

1978: Düsseldorf, Städtische Kunsthalle
Nicolas Poussin 1594-1665 (cat. by P. Rosenberg)

1982: Paris, Grand Palais - New York, The Metropolitan Museum of Art - Chicago, The Art Institute
La peinture française du XVIIe siècle dans les collections américaines. France in the Golden Age (cat. by P. Rosenberg)

1989: Paris, Musée du Louvre
L'inspiration du poète de Poussin. Essai sur l'allégorie du Parnasse. (cat. by M. Fumaroli)

List of illustrations

Principal Museums and Collections

Poussin's pictorial work has been estimated to over two-hundred canvases. Amongst the principal museums in which they can be found, the Louvre, with its thirty-eight paintings, constitutes one of the most important collections today. During the eighteenth century, England acquired a great many of the artist's paintings and hence holds an extensive collection of his work. Thanks to Catherine the Great, Russia also acquired many of his paintings in the eighteenth century, More recently, several American museums have made a number of judicious acquisitions, thereby establishing themselves as now amongst the most important and prestigious holders of Poussin's work.

FRANCE
- *Ajaccio, Musée Fesch*
- *Caen, Musée des Beaux-Arts*
- *Chantilly, Musée Condé*
- *Cherbourg, Musée Thomas-Henry*
- *Montpellier, Musée Fabre*
- *Paris, Louvre*
- *Rouen, Musée des Beaux-Arts*

GERMANY
- *Berlin, Staatliche Museen zu Berlin, Gemäldegalerie*
- *Dresden, Staatliche Kunstsammlungen, Gemäldegalerie*
- *Frankfurt, Städelsches Kunstinstitut und Städlische Galerie*
- *Hanover, Niedersächsische Landesgalerie*
- *Munich, Bayerische Staatsgemäldesammlungen, Alte Pinakothek*

AUSTRALIA
Melbourne, National Gallery of Victoria

AUSTRIA
Vienna, Kunsthistorisches Museum

CANADA
Ottawa, National Gallery of Canada

VATICAN CITY
Vatican, Vatican Museums

SPAIN
Madrid, Museo del Prado

UNITED STATES
- *Boston, Museum of Fine Arts*
- *Cambridge, Fogg Art Museum*
- *Chicago, Art Institute*
- *Cleveland, Museum of Art*
- *Hartford, Wadsworth Atheneum*
- *Minneapolis, Institute of Arts*
- *New York, Metropolitan Museum of Art*
- *Philadelphia, Philadelphia Museum of Art*
- *Washington, National Gallery*

GREAT BRITAIN
- *Birmingham, Barber Institute of Fine Arts*
- *Chatsworth, Duke of Devonshire Collection*
- *Edinburgh, National Gallery of Scotland, Duke of Sutherland Collection*
- *Grantham, Belvoir Castle, Duke of Rutland Collection*
- *Liverpool, Walker Art Gallery, National Museums and Galleries on Merseyside*
- *London, Dulwich College Picture Gallery*
- *London, National Gallery*
- *London, The Wallace Collection*
- *Oxford, Ashmolean Museum*
- *Woburn, Woburn Abbey, Marquis of Tavistock Collection*

REPUBLIC OF IRELAND
- *Dublin, National Gallery of Ireland*

RUSSIA
- *Moscow, Pushkin Museum*
- *St Petersburg, Hermitage Museum*

Table of contents

Set in New Baskerville
Printed and bound in Cordoba, Spain
by Graficromo S.A.
Colour separations by Euroscan, Pantin
and typesetting by Blackjacks, London